DATE			

WHY AIRPLANES FLY

WHY AIRPLANES FLY

By Don Dwiggins

A Golden Gate Junior Book
Childrens Press • Chicago

ACKNOWLEDGEMENTS

The author wishes to thank the many airplane designers and builders who cooperated in making this book. Particular thanks go to Dr. Donald C. Coles, Professor of Aerodynamics at the California Institute of Technology, for his kind guidance and suggestions.

PICTURE CREDITS

All illustrations are by the Author except the following:
Page 16, 17, & 19C: Courtesy Education Development Center, Newton, Mass.
Page 23 Top, 25A and 25B: Federal Aviation Administration.
Page 26: National Aeronautics and Space Administration.
Pages 16, 17, & 19C: Courtesy Education Development Center,

Library of Congress Cataloging in Publication Data

Dwiggins, Don.
  Why airplanes fly.

  "A Golden Gate junior book."
  SUMMARY: Briefly explains the aerodynamic forces that permit airplanes to fly.
  1. Aerodynamics—Juvenile literature. 2. Airplanes—Juvenile literature. [1. Aerodynamics. 2. Airplanes] I. Title.
TL570.D878   629.132'3   76-13503
ISBN 0-516-08889-0

3 4 5 6 7 8 9 10 11 12 13 14 15 16 17 18 19 20 21 R 79 78 77

Have you ever wondered how an airplane weighing thousands of pounds can stay up in air so thin that you can't even feel it or see it? To understand how this is possible, you must know that there are two different kinds of air—calm air and air in motion. Moving air we call Wind. Wind blowing over an airplane's wing is what keeps the plane up. The science of how this works is called *Aerodynamics* (**aer-o-dy-nam-ics**).

5

The Earth really supports this Mooney Super-21 in flight. Read how, below.

Forces in motion are called *Dynamic Forces*. When at work in the sky they are known as *Aerodynamic Forces*. Every time you watch a big plane fly off into "the wild blue yonder" you are watching Aerodynamic Forces in action. The airplane's wing turns the air downward, and the Earth turns it back, so the Earth is really carrying the weight of the airplane in flight.

6

The angle at which the boy's hand meets the Relative Wind (arrow) is called the Angle of Attack.

You can feel the forces of Aerodynamics if you hold your hand outside the window of a moving automobile. If you tilt your hand upward, the wind feels stronger. The same thing happens with an airplane wing.

The angle at which your hand (or the airplane wing) meets the wind is called the *Angle of Attack*. The wind you feel outside the car window is called *Relative Wind*. It feels strong, even on a calm day, because of the car's motion.

7

We are still learning new things about the wind. But how wind blowing over the wing of an airplane produces *Lift* is still as much of a mystery as why a Frisbee flies.

You can send a Frisbee spinning across the sky, to sail so steadily that gusts of wind won't tip it over. Two things help it to fly steady—its spinning motion and its curved shape. When you tip a Frisbee on its side, it looks like an airplane wingtip.

When you throw a Frisbee in still air, the air flowing over it is the *Relative Wind*. Engineers call the Frisbee's spinning motion "Angular Momentum," but that's just their way of saying it goes round and round and remains steady, like a spinning top.

*Smoke trails from wingtips of this stunt plane, a
Super Chipmunk, show how Trailing Vortexes look.*

In the case of an airplane, it is the air, not the plane's
wing, that spins, in small whirlpools called *Vortexes*, or
Vortices. (A *Vortex* is a whirling mass of fluid, such as air
or water.) Some Vortexes form over the wing and are called
Bound Vortexes. Others form behind the wing and at the
wingtips. These are known as *Trailing Vortexes*. (See pp.
24-26.)

Vortexes are born when the airplane's wing shoves the
air downward. This downward shove, which makes the
air spin, is really what causes a plane to stay up. It occurs
because of a principle discovered in the seventeenth century by a famous Englishman, Sir Isaac Newton.

9

This girl is ground-skimming in a hang glider. Her kite sail flies by pushing the air downward. There is more Lift near the ground due to Ground Effect (see Diagram on Page 24).

Newton discovered a law (called the Law of Action and Reaction) which states that *every action has an equal and opposite reaction.* By pushing the air downward, the wing of an airplane gets an equal and opposite push upward. In the same way, when the propeller pushes the air backward, the airplane gets an equal and opposite push forward.

10

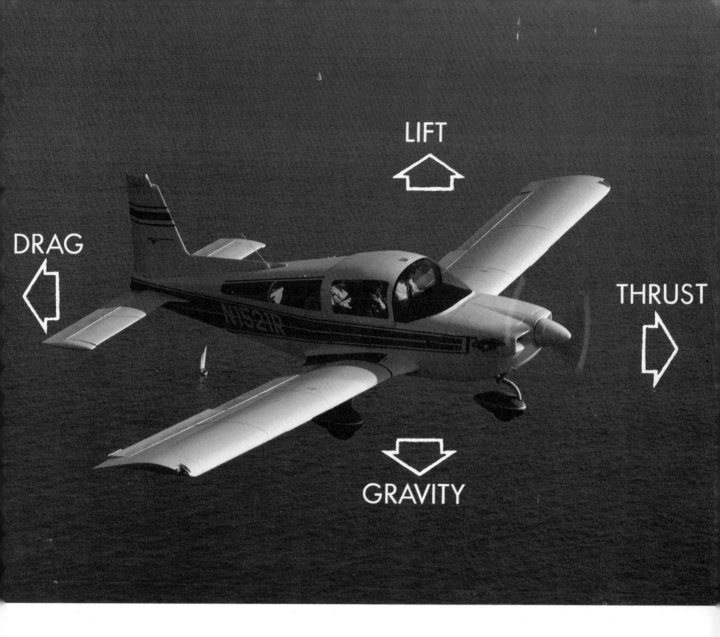

LIFT

DRAG

THRUST

GRAVITY

We call the forward push *Thrust*, and the backward push *Drag*. The plane's wing provides *Lift*, and the Lift must be equal and opposite to the down-pull of *Gravity*. Airplane designers cut down Drag as much as possible, so that the plane's engine can use more energy for making Lift. It does so by pulling the airplane forward. The lower the Drag, the farther the airplane can fly.

11

Seagulls have long, slender wings for soaring flight.

For centuries people wondered how birds could fly without flapping their wings. Birds can soar for hours in rising air currents. Scientists once believed that there was some mysterious energy in the wind, but they didn't know what that energy was. Today we know that there *is* energy in Relative Wind, the force of air in motion.

This girl is launching a model plane with flat wings.

Just how an airplane wing turns this energy into Lift is 13 the secret of flight. Like kites, the earliest airplanes had flat wings which turned the air downward. The wings worked, but not too well. There was too much Drag.

This plane, a Pietenpol Air Camper, has wings curved more on top than on the bottom.

The way that wind blowing over a wing produces Lift is not well understood, even today. Most airplane wings are curved more on top than on the bottom. One theory is that this makes the air flow farther over the top than along the bottom, and so it must flow faster. The faster it flows, the lower the air pressure will be. (According to what is called *Bernoulli's Theorum.*)

14   Air pressure pushes on the wing from both the top and bottom. The pressure on top wants to push the wing down, but the pressure on the bottom is stronger pushing up. The difference in these pushes is the Lift.

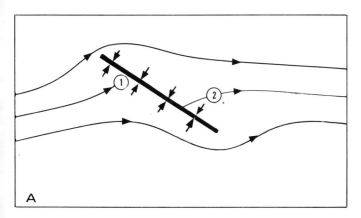
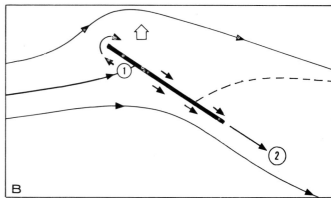

*This is how aerodynamicists explain Bound Vortex. With no air circulation, air pressure over a flat plate is the same on top and bottom. **A:** Wind striking at (1) leaves at (2). **B:** With circulation added, Relative Wind blows smoothly from (1) and leaves trailing edge at (2). This is called d'Alembert's Paradox.*

Another theory explains Lift in a different way. Early in this century two scientists noticed that air blowing over a lifting wing flowed sharply upward and spun around the front edge of the wing. Then it flowed smoothly off the wing at the rear. They called this flow the *Bound Vortex,* because it was bound to the wing. It also flowed outward along the wing to the wingtips, with the air spinning faster over the top of the wing and more slowly along the bottom.

You can easily see how a Vortex works by filling your bathtub with water, then pulling the plug. The water in the tub will spin around and around in a Vortex as it empties out into the drain.

15

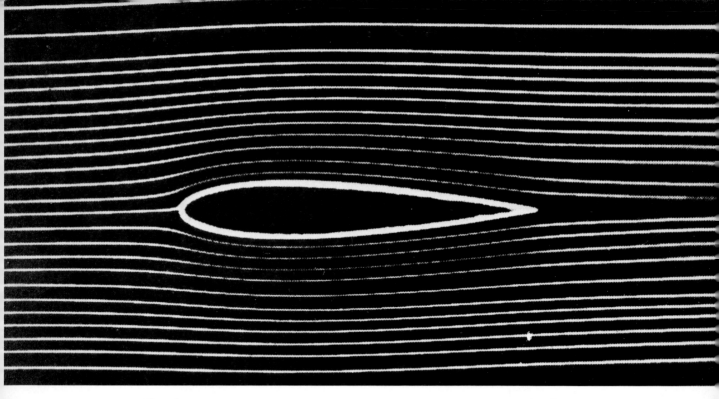

Smokestreams in wind tunnel blowing over a wing with the same curve on top and bottom. At zero Angle of Attack there is no Lift.

The science of Aerodynamics is hard to understand because air is invisible. We can't actually *see* what is happening. But there are ways we *can* see Aerodynamics at work. One way is to place a model airplane in a wind tunnel and blow thin streams of smoke over it. A wind tunnel is a long box with a blower at one end and a window on the side. When the smoke is turned on, we can see smoke streams blowing over the model's wing.

16

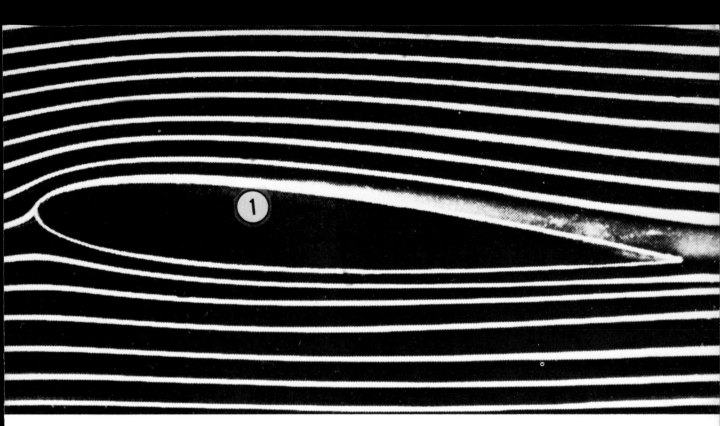

Same wing in wind tunnel tilted upward, with small Angle of Attack. Lift results from lower pressure area on top. Boundary Layer flow on top is Laminar to (1), called the Separation Point, and Turbulent behind.

Tests in smoke tunnels show that flat wings do not work as well as curved wings, like those of a bird. Curved wings produce more Lift and less Drag—but why? The secret lies in the thin film of air flowing next to the wing's surface. It is called the *Boundary Layer*. This layer can be as thin as a playing card.

If the air flowing over the wing is smooth, it is called *Laminar Flow*. If it burbles and tumbles about, it is called *Turbulent Flow*. A rough wing surface can cause Turbulent Flow in the Boundary Layer. This is known as *Skin-Friction Drag*. When it happens, the Boundary Layer is said to become *Viscous*, or sticky. (The word viscous comes from the Latin word *viscum*, for mistletoe, whose white berries are sticky.)

17

This race pilot glued wool tufts all over his Smith Miniplane racer to check for unwanted Drag (left). In flight, the tufts flow straight back. This shows the airflow is smooth, or Laminar, over whole plane.

In addition to smoke tunnel tests, there is another way to see Aerodynamics at work. Wool tufts are attached to a real airplane's wing. If the tufts lie back flat when the plane is in flight, we know that the airflow is Laminar. If the tufts jump around, the airflow is Turbulent.

Sometimes the Boundary Layer separates from the plane's wing. This airflow separation destroys the wing's Lift, and the wing is said to *Stall*.

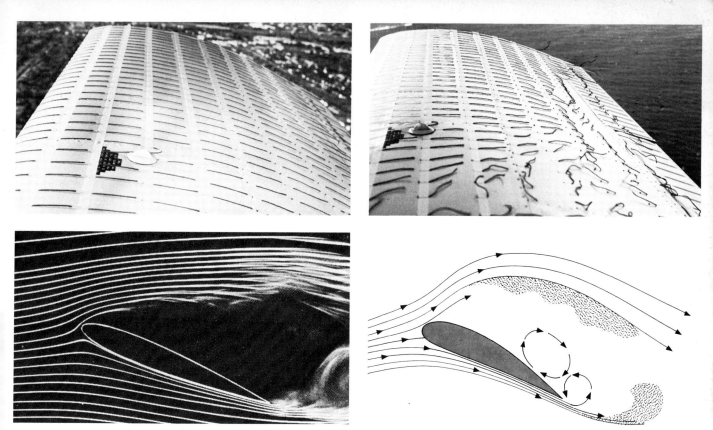

Wool tufts on this wing (upper left) lie flat until the wing begins to stall (upper right). Notice how tufts blow forward at trailing edge. Wind tunnel smokestreams (lower left) show boundary layer separation in a stall, with Trailing Vortex behind. Diagram (lower right) shows how Vortexes form over wing in a stall.

If the wing should stall, we would see something strange happen. By watching wool tufts on the top surface of a real wing, we would see tiny Vortexes curl up around the wing's trailing edge.

When a stall happens, the wool tufts (or the smoke streams) sometimes blow forward instead of backward. This reverse flow shows us that turbulent Vortexes are forming on top of the wing. The Vortexes finally force the laminar airflow to separate from all but the front part of the wing. Then the lower pressure area above the wing is lost and Lift is destroyed. This is called the Stall point.

19

Sometimes airplane designers use special slots and flaps on a wing to give it more curve. A curved wing can fly slower, at a higher angle of attack without stalling, because the airflow does not separate from the wing.

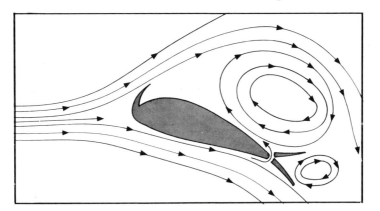

One recent idea in airplane design is to fit the wing with a front flap (called a *Vortex Generator*), and split flaps at the rear. These flaps give a smoother Bound Vortex at a higher Angle of Attack, so the airplane can land almost straight down, like a bird.

This airplane, the VariEze, is made entirely of glass. Tiny winglets at tips of slender wings are Whitcomb vortex diffusers, added to cut Induced Drag. Front control surface is called a Canard.

Airplanes that fly fast have thinner wings than airplanes that fly slow. Airplanes with long, slender wings, like those on sailplanes, can fly farther. This is because long, slender wings produce less of what is called *Induced Drag.*

Induced Drag is different from Skin-Friction Drag. It results from the action of the wind in producing Lift. Let's look for a moment at how this works.

21

This Cessna 170, taking off from Saline Valley Airstrip, is flying in Ground Effect, blowing dust.

22   When an airplane on the ground starts to move forward, the air underneath it is shoved downward, near the trailing edge of the wing. This makes a whirlpool of air behind the wing, called a *Starting Vortex*. You can see it if you watch dust blowing hard behind an airplane when it starts to roll.

Flying near the ground, as on takeoff and landing, trailing Vortexes behind the wing push against the earth. This gives the wing more Lift, so the airplane can fly slower than it could higher up. This is called flying in *Ground Effect*. Pelicans fly in Ground Effect when they skim the waves without flapping their wings.

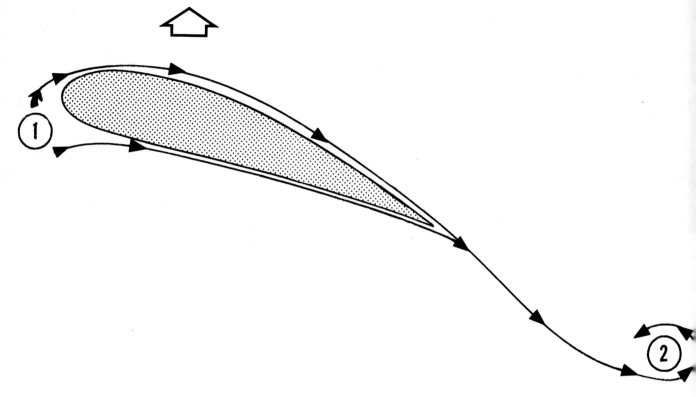

The Circulation Theory of Lift. In 1905 two men named Kutta and Zhukovski discovered how a Bound Vortex starts at (1), and ends in a Trailing Vortex at (2). Near the ground, the air has something hard to push against, so the wing gets more Lift.

In nature, a Vortex cannot be created without another forming, of equal strength and opposite direction. This is according to the Law of Action and Reaction. The opposite of a Starting Vortex becomes the Bound Vortex, which is bound to the wing.

Jet plane flying past colored smoke tower creates a Vortex like a small tornado. Below, a wingtip vortex diffuser, invented by Dr. Richard T. Whitcomb. The tiny fin below the rudder slows down tip Vortex, reducing Induced Drag.

The air pressure is higher under the wing than above it, so the air wants to flow around the wingtips from bottom to top. This produces a *Trailing Vortex* at the wingtip. The complete circulation of Vortexes around the wing is what makes Lift.

25

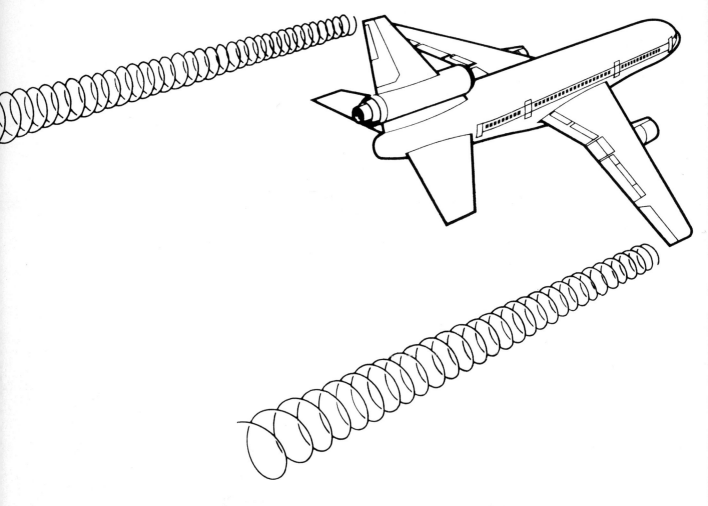

This diagram shows how wingtip Vortexes form behind a heavy jet. Such small tornadoes can flip a light plane upside down, should it fly behind a jet.

To fly, heavy airplanes need more Lift than light planes. Extra Lift means that Vortexes are bigger and also spin faster. Trailing Vortexes behind heavy jets are dangerous. They have the strength of small tornadoes, and can flip a small plane upside down.

26

This plane, a Maule M-5, flies over Mt. Whitney.

Airplanes that fly high in the sky fly in thin air. The Skin Friction Drag is less at high altitudes, and so they can go faster with the same power. At 18,000 feet the air is only half as dense (heavy) as at sea level.

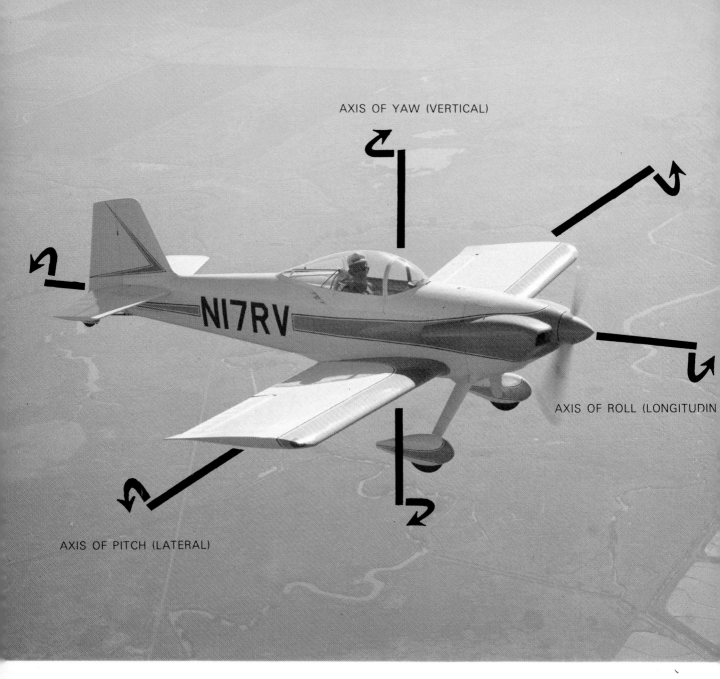

AXIS OF YAW (VERTICAL)

AXIS OF ROLL (LONGITUDIN

AXIS OF PITCH (LATERAL)

Pilots must have control of their airplanes in three ways —forward, sideways, and up and down. We call those controls longitudinal, lateral, and vertical *Axes*. The airplane movements around these Axes are called *Pitch*, *Roll*, and *Yaw*.

28

This aerobatic biplane, an Acroduster I, can roll completely around in less than two seconds.

Control surfaces on the wings, called *Ailerons*, make the airplane roll about its longitudinal axis. Elevator surfaces on the tail provide Pitch control around the lateral axis. The plane's rudder produces Yaw about the vertical axis. But the pilot doesn't use the rudder to turn an airplane, as in a boat. Instead, he turns by rolling the airplane into a bank. (Some modern plane designers think rudders are not necessary; birds don't have rudders, of course.)

Some planes are designed to fly slow, not fast. This one, called VariViggen, will not stall. Its elevators and ailerons are up front, on the little wing called a Canard.

Airplanes with special thin wings and powerful jet engines can fly faster than sound. But the real challenge is to make airplanes fly slower, not faster. Maybe some day we'll find a way to make an airplane stop, back up, or land gently straight down, like a seagull.

30

This sport plane, called the PDQ-2, weighs barely more than the pilot.

Many young people are now designing and building their own airplanes, in home workshops and in schools. Some grade school teachers help their students to design and build real airplanes that fly well.

Today, the sky beckons to young people more strongly than ever before. Men have landed on the Moon, but wouldn't it be more fun to land your own airplane in a treetop, like a bird?

31

Have you ever wondered how an airplane weighing thousands of pounds can stay up in air so thin that you can't even feel it or see it? To understand how this is possible, you must know that there are two different kinds of air — calm air and air in motion. Moving air we call wind. Wind blowing over an airplane's wing is what keeps the plane up.

This thought-provoking book for young readers is a fascinating introduction to the science of Aerodynamics in terms of airplanes and why they fly, written simply and clearly by an author who knows his subject from a wealth of first-hand experience. Mr. Dwiggins uses a minimum of technical language in explaining basic Aerodynamic principles and illuminates even the most complex concepts with easily understood examples from everyday life. Like its companion book, *Why Kites Fly, Why Airplanes Fly* is lavishly illustrated with exciting photographs of planes in flight and on the ground as well as with many graphic explanatory diagrams and drawings.

Don Dwiggins has been a flight instructor for more than thirty-five years and has logged well over 10,000 hours as a first pilot. He was an instructor in Britain's Royal Air Force in World War II and from there went on to a distinguished career both as an airman and as a writer on aviation subjects. He was aviation editor of two major metropolitan newspapers and has contributed thousands of articles on flying to national magazines. In addition, he has written many successful books for young people, among them *Why Kites Fly* and *The Sky Is Yours*, published by Childrens Press, *Eagle Has Landed*, *Voices In The Sky* and *Spaceship Earth*. Mr. Dwiggins, who flys his own plane, is presently senior editor of the magazine, *Plane and Pilot*. He makes his home in Malibu, California.